How To Master Investing in Crypto Currencies

Table of Contents

Disclaimer: 3
Introduction 4
SECTION 1: Getting Started 5
Please Stop Reading the Headlines… 6
    Key Takeaways: 12
    Action Steps: 12
What is a Market Cycle? 13
    How Many Market Cycles has Bitcoin Had Since 2009? 19
The Bell Curve of Bitcoin and the Cryptocurrency Chasm 23
    The Bitcoin Bell Curve 24
        The Innovators: 24
        Early Adopters: 24
        Key Takeaways: 26
        Action Steps: 26
        Key Takeaways: 27
        Action Steps: 28
SECTION #2: How to Create a Crypto Investment Plan 29
    Creating a Crypto Investment Plan 31
        Defining Your Risk Tolerance 32
Wealth Accumulation Goals 33
    Wealth Accumulation Goals Questionnaire: 34
    Does Your Current Lifestyle Support Your Crypto Goals? 35
    Performance Expectations 36
    Paying Taxes 36
    What is your Investment Criteria? 37
How to Create the Best Portfolio Allocation for You: 39
    Tier 1: Blue Chip Cryptos: 39
    Tier 2: Penny Cryptos: 39
    Tier 3: ICO Initial Coin Offerings: 39

Key Takeaways: 41

Suggested Actions: 41

SECTION #3: How to Trade Without Emotion and Make Consistent Returns 42

MAKE YOUR TRADES SMALL 42

If You Can Make Money in Small Amounts, Then Why Are Many Traders Impatient? 44

The Worst Mistake Any Crypto Trader Can Make 45

How Much is Too Much? 47

Key Takeaways: 49

Action Steps: 49

10 Reasons Crypto Traders Make Money 50

Key Takeaways: 53

Action Steps: 53

Can You Predict the Future Price Movements in the Crypto market? The Answer will Surprise You! 54

What is Technical Analysis? 54

Key Takeaways: 55

Action Steps: 55

The #1 Reason to Lose Money When Trading Cryptos 56

Are You Overactive? 56

Why is it a bad idea to overtrade your account? 57

Key Takeaways: 57

Action Steps: 57

Take the Money and Run 58

How to Create a Crypto Withdrawal Plan 60

Crypto Withdrawal Plan: 60

Resource Section: 62

Disclaimer:

The information in this course is for educational purposes only. The information is not financial, trading or tax advice or recommendations. The publisher and author bear no responsibility or control over the actions of those who take this course. Cryptocurrencies are a very high degree of risk. Trading or investing in cryptocurrencies is one of the highest risk any investor can take. Past results are not indicative of future returns.

The indicators and strategies mentioned in this course are for educational purposes only and should not be construed as investment advice. The publisher and author does not warrant its completeness or accuracy or warrant any results from the use of the information.

The reader uses the information in this course at their own risk and it is their sole responsibility. The reader needs to evaluate the accuracy, completeness and usefulness of the information.

You must assess the risk of trading cryptocurrencies with your broker and tax advisor. The reader must make their own independent decisions regarding any strategies mentioned.

The reader isn't guaranteed of any profit, making money and may even loss all of their money. The readers trading strategies may be consistent or inconsistent with the information provided.

Introduction

In this book, you will learn the skills needed to become a successful and disciplined crypto trader. I will share with you the very same strategies and techniques that have made me and my clients a lot of money. You see, prior to getting involved in cryptocurrency and blockchain in 2013, I spent 15 years as a registered investment advisor, series 7 stockbroker and mutual fund wholesaler.

I have worked with and had one-on-one discussions with some of the top money managers in the world including Louis Navellier, Bill Gross from Pimco, money managers at Fidelity, the Bank of New York Mellon and many others.

Since starting my investment career in 1994, I have seen all kinds of markets including the Internet boom and bust in the late 1990's, the banking crisis of 2008 and now the crypto markets. Experiencing these markets firsthand has provide valuable insight and knowledge that can only be learned by living through these events.

The strategies included in this book have been proven to work very well and I am going to share them with you!

SECTION 1: Getting Started

The purpose of this book isn't to provide specific time sensitive trading information or how to use technical analysis indicators or specific trading ideas and tips. I offer other courses and step-by-step videos that provide up to the minute market insight, "look over my shoulder" real-time trading strategies, courses on technical analysis, in-depth portfolio allocation strategies and more. I'll share more about these other courses in the resource section at the end of this book.

The purpose of this book is to provide you with a solid foundation to be a successful long-term crypto trader. Being a successful trader isn't about having the best technical analysis skills or the best price tracking software. It's about the ability to control your emotions while trading and following a well-defined and disciplined investment strategy.

Having this foundation, you'll learn not only how to survive a crypto bear market and crypto crash but how to profit from it when the market rebounds. You'll also learn how to squeeze the maximum profit out of the market during a crypto bull run.

Best of all, crypto is here to stay. We are still at the very early stages of mass adoption of cryptos and blockchain. This means, you still have time to position your portfolio to take advantage of the potential massive gains in the near future. Just think of what you can do once you know how to get in on the ground floor in this upcoming crypto bull market!

Let's go ahead and get started.

Please Stop Reading the Headlines…

The first thing to remember is when it comes to investing - it doesn't matter if it is stocks, bonds, real estate or cryptos - history always repeats itself. In fact, many of the same headlines about a bull market, bear market, market crash, market bubble that are making the front page of Yahoo, blogs, newspapers and magazines are almost identical to those headlines from the internet boom and bust of the 1990's.

One thing to keep in mind when reading headlines is that the purpose of sensational headlines is to sell newspapers, magazines or to get you to "click" the headline and visit their website. It is not to provide the highest quality of insight or guidance for trading crypto currencies.

Let's take a look at a few past and present sensational headlines:

#1: *Dow Industrial Top 10000 – If This Is a Bubble, It Sure is Hard to Pop*. March 30, 1999 – Wall Street Journal   (Source: Google Images)

#2: *Bitcoin's price swings wildly, touching above $19,000* - December 7, 2017 – LaTimes   (Source: LATimes.com)

#3: *Bitcoin is Dead* – March 5, 2014 – The Weekly Standard

Bitcoin Is Dead

JONATHAN V. LAST @JVLAST | 5 MIN READ

March 5, 2014 11:35 AM

"Bitcoin" is the most widespread, cryptographically-secure Internet currency. It was created in 2009 by someone (or someones) who referred to themselves as "Satoshi Nakamoto." Once it was released into the wild, the bitcoin currency ecosystem operated on a public, inalterable schedule. We know exactly how many bitcoins there are in existence today () and how many there will eventually be in total: when the 21 millionth bitcoin is minted, the plates automatically self-destruct. (This is a metaphor, of course. There are no minting "plates," and nothing's going to actually explode.) If you want to read the whole Wikipedia entry on bitcoin, have at it.

#4: *The Craziest Bubble Ever* – July 27, 2017 – Forbes   (Source: Forbes)

#5: *Bitcoin Trades Full Speed Ahead* – June 7, 2017 – Wall Street Journal (Source: Google Images)

I can provide dozens of other examples, but you get the point. These sensational headlines are meant to stir up your emotions and could get you to take action that may not be in your best interest. Read the articles, but the point is - DON'T to get caught up in the sensational headlines! Read the article, but don't make investment decisions on what you read in a newspaper article, in a forum or in a magazine.

The most important part the majority of these articles usually miss is teaching you what to do with the information in the article. The author fails to provide an action plan to profit from the information in the article. They are simply stating facts and sometimes those facts aren't even well researched.

For example, the next time you read an article, either online or in a newspaper or in a magazine about the crypto, look to see if the article provides a specific plan of action on what to do with the information found in the article. Does the article provide time-tested strategies you can use to profit from the information in the article or does it simply state facts? Finally, look to see if the sources used in the article are credible.

Key Takeaways:

- History always repeats itself. While the markets may have different players and different investments, the game is always the same. If you learn how to spot these repeating trends you can make a lot money.
- The purpose of sensational headlines is to sell magazines or newspapers or get you to visit a website.
- Don't take any action without in-depth research on any information from an article, blog post or forum post.

Action Steps:

- When reading articles, be on the lookout for action steps provided by the author on the information in the article. If action steps aren't included in the article, write down at least one action step you can take.

For example, if the article is about how the price of Bitcoin is continuing to decline, your action step could be to look at the daily price chart of Bitcoin to see if the price is currently reaching any support levels. If so, you might be able to take a new position and take advantage of the upcoming rebound in price.

What is a Market Cycle?

A market cycle is a long-term pattern of prices. Understanding market cycles are key to taking advantage of pending opportunities or avoiding potential market pullbacks. Market cycles help you to identify repeating cycles or price patterns.

In addition, market cycles are also related to the underlying emotions of the investors in the marketplace. Market cycles often reflect the underlying fear and/or greed of the overall market.

Check out this market cycle chart showing price movement with overlays of market awareness and the emotions of fear and/or greed.

Each market cycle is made up of four distinctive stages that are defined in the chart below as:

- Stealth Phase or Smart Money
- Awareness or Institutional Investors
- Mania Phase or Public Involvement
- Blow Off Phase or Public Disillusion

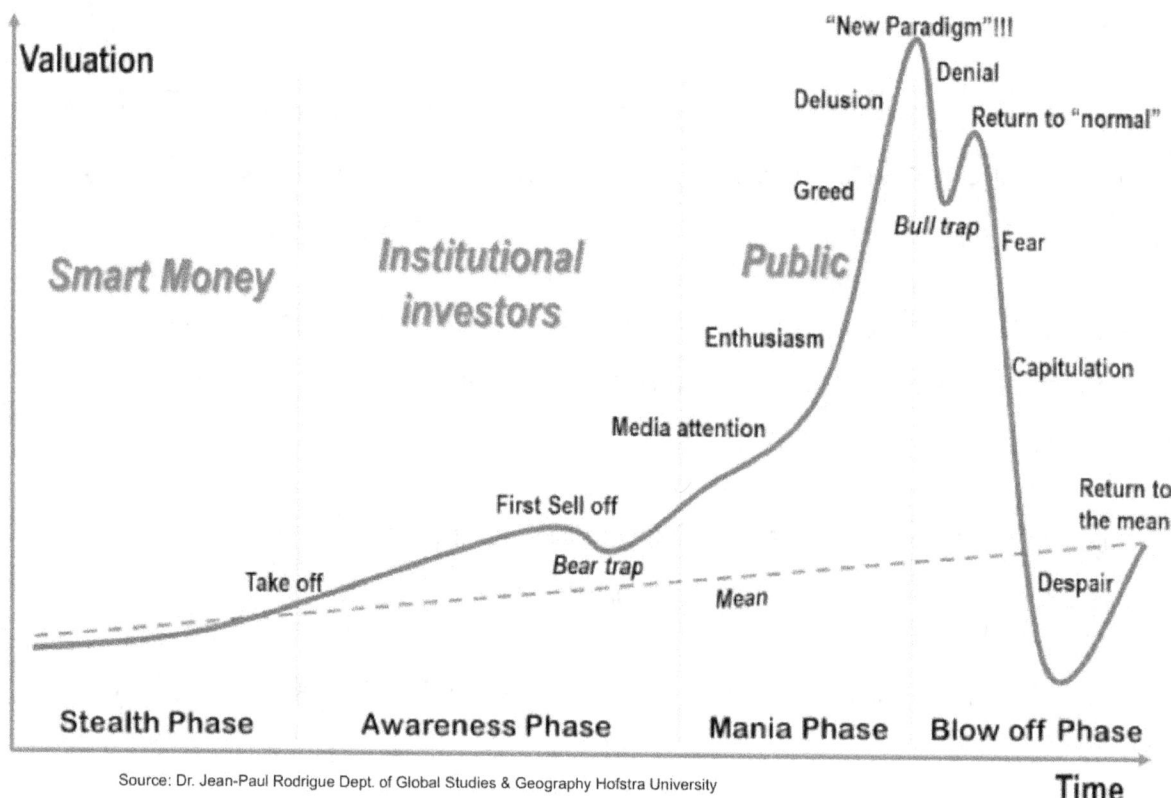

Source: Dr. Jean-Paul Rodrigue Dept. of Global Studies & Geography Hofstra University

Let's learn more about each stage of a market as defined in the chart above and as it related to the price of Bitcoin:

The Stealth Phase or Smart Money:

During this first phase of a market cycle, usually only individuals or companies involved in the sector are familiar with the emerging new technology or product. As outlaying websites and forums begin to increase public awareness about bitcoin and cryptocurrencies, prices begin to increase. This leads to the phase two.

The Awareness Phase or Institutional Money:

During this second phase, astute institutional investors begin to take notice. It was during this phase that venture capitalist Tim Draper placed the winning bid for 29,656 bitcoins auctioned off in July, 2014 by the U.S. Marshals. In July of 2014, the price of bitcoin was about $450.

The Manic Phase or Public Involvement:

The third phase of a market cycle is when the public received the first real introduction to bitcoin and cryptocurrencies. During the last few months of 2017, it seemed like almost every time you turned on the television or visited a website, you would see a story about bitcoin and cryptos.

Due to the massive amounts of money flowing into the market and the FOMO (fear of missing out), this phase experiences exponential price increases. You can see the price spike on the above chart. Similar price movement occurred on the chart of the NASDAQ during the months prior to the dot com crash.

The Blow Off Phase or Public Disillusion:

The forth phase of a market cycle is the top of the market. It commonly referred to as a "blow off top". After prices reach ultimate resistance levels they begin to fall. As they fall, novice investors and those who bought at the top of the market begin to panic and sell. Thus, driving prices down faster and further than they normally would. This causes many in the investing public to be disillusioned about the future of bitcoin and cryptocurrencies.

After a bottom of the market is found, prices begin to return back to the mean.

Now, check out at the actual daily price chart of Bitcoin dating back to the beginning of 2017.

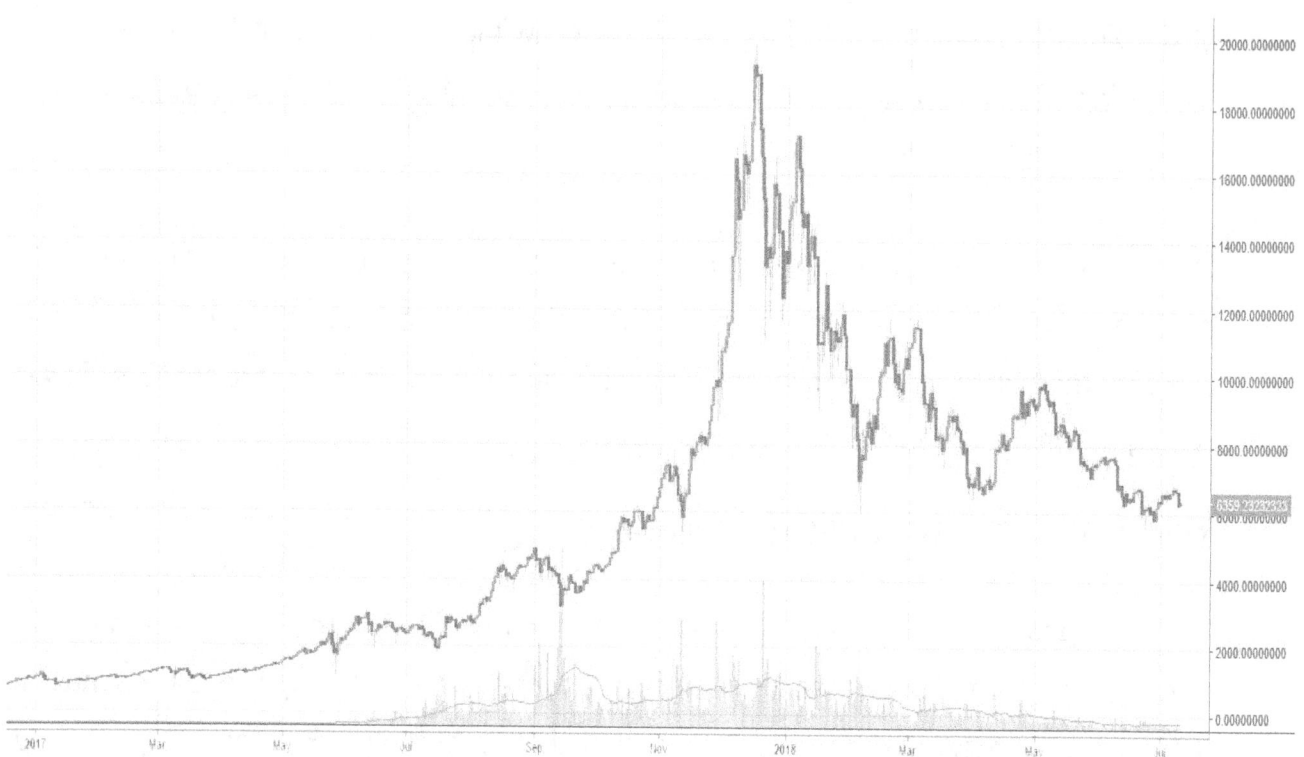

In comparison, the bitcoin price chart and market cycle chart look similar.

In the Bitcoin chart, the market topped in December of 2017 at almost $20,000 USD and then continued to drop to around $6,000 USD to July of 2018. That is a huge drop. As outlined in the market cycle chart, I believe we are near the bottom of the current cycle. Prices should begin to rebound during the summer months of 2018.

Even if we drop another 10% at this point, it's really not going to make that much of a difference. I mean if you started with $200,000 and your portfolio is now worth $60,000, will another $6,000 decline really make a difference to your portfolio right now?

I'm not making light of the situation. The market has declined over 70%, but I am suggesting to look at the market as what it is and not what you want it to be.

Let me explain...

In this example, let's say you invested $200,000 at the top of the market and you may have decided to sell if the value of your portfolio went to $150,000. A $50,000 USD was your maximum loss you would be willing to accept when you opened your initial position. So you placed stop losses that sold out at $150,000 USD.

However, many traders aren't disciplined to set stop losses when they first enter a trade. The majority don't follow and implement a predetermined Crypto Investment Plan. An investment plan is a well-thought investment strategy to provide you parameters for your trades. Having a predetermined plan will help you to make well-informed decisions for your portfolio.

This is important...

If you currently don't have such a plan for your portfolio and the overall market is declining and just your positions, it is usually best to ride out the bear market. In addition, if there is no substantial news about your positions it is usually best to wait for the market to recover.

One of the main reasons investors lose money in a bear market is they sell after the crash actually happened. They don't wait for the recovery, and that makes all the difference!

Many investors don't fully understand market fluctuations and market cycles. They watch the market going down day after day. They watch the value of their portfolio getting crushed and after they reach a certain amount of pain, they panic sell in despair. This is known a capitulation, see the market cycle chart, and it usually signals the bottom of the market cycle.

After capitulation, the market usually has a massive rebound and starts to recover. This is especially true in the crypto market. Those who sold near the bottom are now regretting their decision and rush to get back into the market.

This is the very same approach many of the top money managers and experienced crypto traders follow on a daily basis. They make decisions based upon where the marketing is moving toward, not where it is on a given day.

If investors made a purchase during the "greed" stage of the market, see market cycle chart above, and now find the value of their portfolio underwater, they need to take a step back and re-evaluate the fundamentals. Think of the emotions and analytical reasons that caused them to make the investment in the first place. The most important part of this evaluation is to determine what part of the market cycle they are in.

If the current market indicates it is near the bottom of the cycle and you opened your positions at higher prices, the best plan of action is usually to do nothing. Let the market recover and enjoy the rebound.

How Many Market Cycles has Bitcoin Had Since 2009?

Let's take a look at a chart of the Bitcoin.

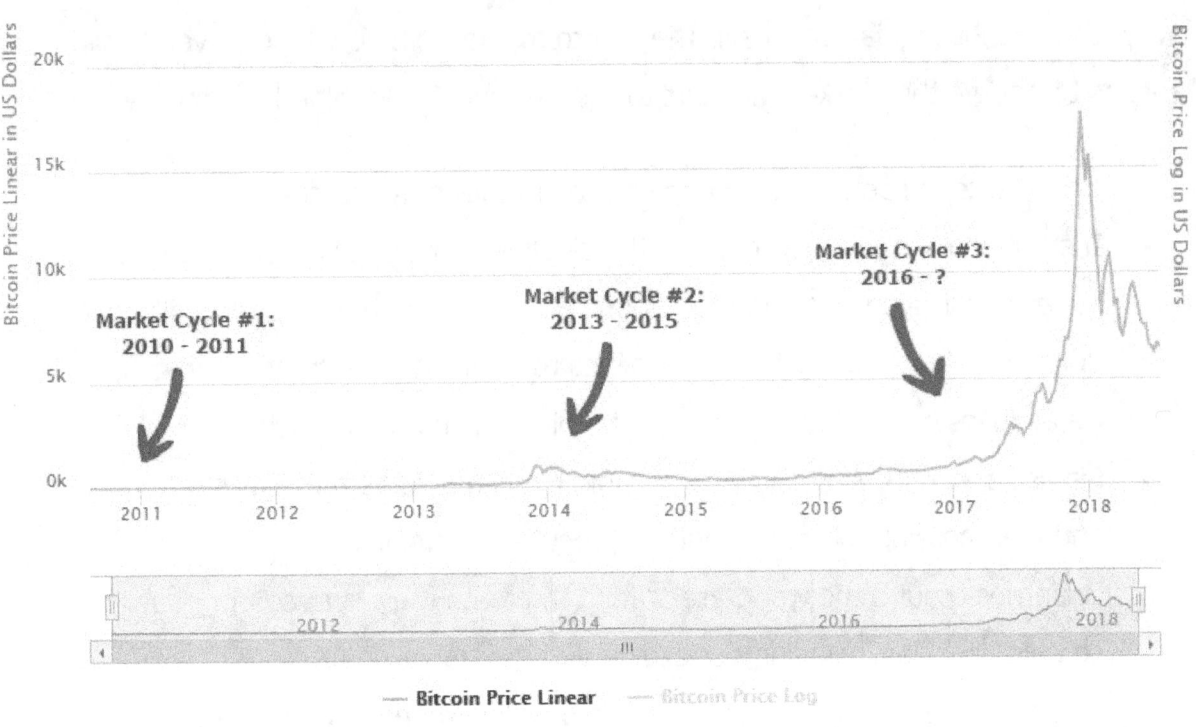

Bitcoin has had 3 market cycles since its creation in 2009.

- Market Cycle #1: 2010 – 2011 – Price movement from $.07 USD to $22.59 USD before pulling back.
- Market Cycle #2: 2013 – 2015 – Price movement from $42.36 USD to $945 USD before pulling back.
- Market Cycle #3: 2016 - ? – Price movement from $376 to $19,783 USD before pulling back. This cycle is still in progress. However, I believe we are at the bottom and waiting for a recovery.

The biggest concern during the first few crypto crashes was if bitcoin, blockchain and crypto would survive in the future. Would bitcoin and cryptocurrencies be able to deliver in their promise. But now that question is answered, since it is obvious that bitcoin, crypto and blockchain are here to stay. It is just a matter of when the crypto market will start to recover.

Unlike the previous initial crashes in the crypto market, we now have several solid reasons to believe the market will start to recover and I've outlined them for you:

- Wider acceptance of Bitcoin and cryptocurrencies by merchants.
- Institutional money is waiting on the sidelines until bitcoin gets a little more government oversight and regulation. This will allow hundreds of millions of dollars currently sitting on the sidelines to pour into the crypto market.
- Retail investors are more aware of bitcoin and cryptocurrencies.
- Mainstream television shows and cable news networks are now starting to review and talk more about bitcoin and cryptocurrencies daily.
- Countries around the world are stating to create their own country-specific cryptocurrencies including Venezuela and Russia.
- Blockchain technology is rapidly being developed and implemented across industries including logistics, finance and more.

For example, in 2013, Bitcoin jumped from $100 to over $1,000 and then pulled back to around $200. For those in the market at the time, it was considered to be a massive crash. However, in the longer-term market cycle, it was a small retrenchment.

The 2018 crypto bear market is just another market cycle. When we lookback and review the charts in a few years from now, the 2018 pull back will be small compared the future price of Bitcoin and other blue chip cryptocurrencies.

I believe we are still at the very beginnings of the crypto and blockchain mass adoption. We have experienced a bear market in crypto markets over the past several months, but in the grand scheme of things the next crypto bull market will wildly exceed our expectations. In comparison, I believe Bitcoin, crypto and blockchain can be compared to the internet in the early 90's before it had mass adoption.

Mass adoption is the key to crypto success. Just like the market cycle of bitcoin, the mass adoption of new technology also has a market cycle. I am going to share with you one of the best resources to learn how new technology is accepted in to the marketplace. This will help you to see the huge wealth accumulation potential offered by bitcoin and cryptocurrencies.

Also, if you notice, the majority of "crypto expert" YouTube personalities aren't talking about the life cycle of bitcoin technology or how this technology is starting to weave its way into our daily lives. The videos they create are usually only about current price movement of a specific cryptocurrency or bitcoin.

One of the reasons these "crypto gurus" only talk about daily price movement is they haven't lived through a full market cycle. They don't have the financial training or life experience to draw from. Many of them simply haven't taken the time to thoroughly learn the history of how new technology is adopted by the masses.

Many crypto gurus simply want to sell you something. With this course, and my history and expertise, you now proven insight and experience regarding crypto. When you think about, isn't that what you really want? A proven guide to help educate you and help you avoid the pitfalls of investing into crypto?

If you really want to know how technology achieves mass adoption, get of copy of the book by Geoffrey Moore, entitled *Crossing the Chasm*. It is a step-by-step guide how to market new technology to the mass market.

Source: Google Images

I first read *Crossing the Chasm* in the mid-1990's when I started my investment advisory career. The wisdom found in this book helped me to make a lot money for myself and my clients during the Internet boom of the 90's. It also saved me a lot of money during the bust. The reason is it provided insight into the understanding of technology market cycles.

The Bell Curve of Bitcoin and the Cryptocurrency Chasm

According to Geoffrey A. Moore (*Crossing the Chasm*), the technology adoption life cycle has five groups. These groups are:

- Innovators
- Early Adopters
- Early Majority
- Late Majority
- Laggards

The Technology Adoption Life Cycle Bell Curve looks like:

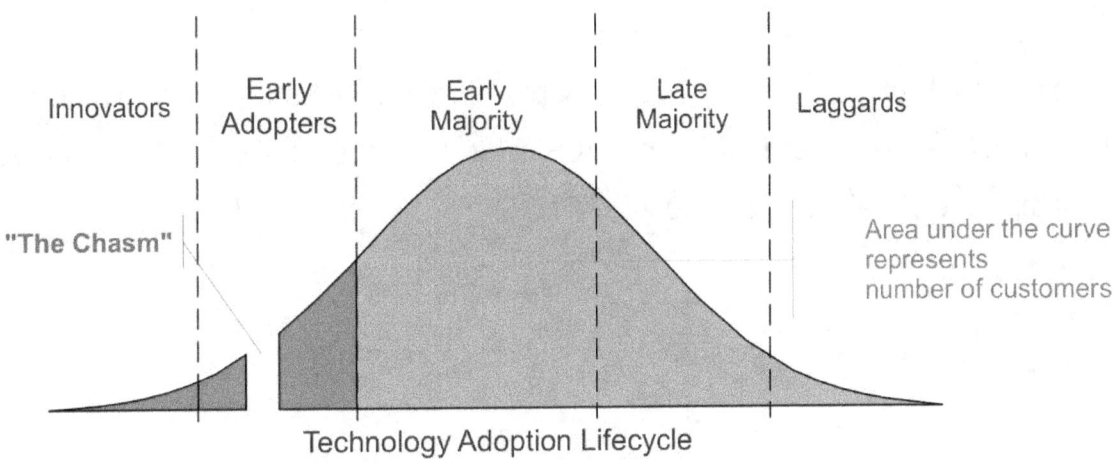

Source: Wikipedia

The Bitcoin Bell Curve

The Technology Adoption Life Cycle Bell Curve can easily be applied to bitcoin and cryptocurrency. We can easily image the same chart to being used to explain the mass adoption cycle of bitcoin and cryptocurrency.

With that being said, we can state we are at the beginning of the **Bitcoin Bell Curve.** Since we are still in the beginning stages, at this time, it only makes sense to learn more about the first groups that are located on the left side of the bell curve.

The Innovators:

The innovators in the crypto realm were those individuals and development teams in 2008 who continued the study of blockchain and began development of many of the cryptocurrencies we are familiar with today soon after when the Bitcoin whitepaper was published.

And don't forget, the early bitcoin miners supporting the network. This group also includes the legendary individual who purchased two pizzas for 10,000 BTC to prove the eco-system offers real world solutions!

Early Adopters:

As we move up the bell curve, the early adopters are the next group. These are the individuals further embracing the underlying technology and helping to move it into the marketplace. This includes those of you taking this course. You are part of the very early adopters and that group has great company. You are making history.

As indicated, by the chart above, soon after the early adopters begin to embrace bitcoin and the underlying technology, a chasm is found. I would like to refer to this as the "Bitcoin Chasm".

As described in Moore's book, the chasm is described as "separates the early adopters from the majority". This is the most unforgiving transition in the entire technology adoption life cycle.

This definition suggests the underlying "technology" has shown little or no commercial success. The technology I am specifically referring to relates to bitcoin, cryptocurrencies and blockchain.

In early 2017, many of the news articles, blog posts, and television and radio interviews discussed "price movement" of bitcoin and other cryptocurrencies. However, most didn't address the underlying technology of blockchain and cryptocurrencies and how they related to each other.

Today, however, more and more websites, blogs and newspapers are writing about how cryptocurrencies and blockchain are being used in real world situations to solve real world issues. This shows how the underlying technology is actually showing more and more commercial success.

Here are only a few examples of how crypto is confidentially is moving through the unforgiving chasm of this early life cycle.

- Country specific crypto currencies: Venezuela and Russia have created their own national cryptocurrencies.
- Real World Usage: Cryptocurrencies like Basic Attention Token (BAT) is solving the problem of how musicians, authors and video producers get paid without a third-party.
- MasterCard recently announced they received a patent for blockchain-based payment options. This simply means you may be able to pay for goods and services with your bitcoin holdings using Mastercard.
- The strategic partnership between IBM and Stellar Lumens (XLM) recently announced they are working on a "Crypto Dollar". The goal is to offer a stable

coin that operates on the Stellar network. This would make it easier to make blockchain-based payments.

While bitcoin, cryptocurrencies and blockchain still have to make more headway prior to mass adoption, these advancements bode well for this upcoming technology in the future. That is why I firmly believe are still are the very early stages of the bell curve and moving through the Bitcoin Chasm toward mass adoption.

Key Takeaways:

- History always repeats itself.
- Market cycles represent the psychology of the investors within a specific market.
- Bitcoin, blockchain and cryptocurrencies are currently in the "Chasm" of the bell curve.
- Mass adoption of bitcoin, blockchain and cryptocurrencies are needed to get out of the "Bitcoin Chasm".

Action Steps:

- Read the book, *Crossing the Chasm* by Geoffrey A. Moore.

How to be a Successful Long-Term Crypto Trader – The Answer Will Surprise You!

The answer may surprise you. It is usually the last thing crypto traders learn or even consider. However, it should be the first since it is most vital to becoming a successful crypto trader and investor.

The answer to becoming a successful long-term crypto investor is not learning how to read charts or improve your technical analysis skills. It's not reading the crypto forums or even watching the so-called crypto gurus on YouTube.

The first step to becoming a successful long-term crypto investor is to avoid trading with emotion. Avoiding emotional trading is vital to your long-term success!

A good way to avoid trading with emotion is not to read the headlines every 15 minutes or worry about daily events. However, you shouldn't be complacent either. Before the crypto market topped out in early 2018, many investors especially new crypto investors, probably never read about market cycles. They may have not realized markets can decline in value and when they do decline, it can be a very nasty correction.

When the market started to decline, many new crypto investors started to panic sell, thus driving the market down faster and further than it would have otherwise.

Key Takeaways:
- Don't make trades based upon emotions.
- Avoid emotional extremes that may occur after reading a sensational article on why you should buy or sell a specific crypto currency
- Only read trusted crypto news sources.
- Market cycles represent the psychology of the investors within a specific market.

Action Steps:

- Follow only 2 or 3 reputable crypto websites for your crypto news.
- Avoid crypto forums since many of the other people on the forums are either trying to pump coins or they don't know what they are talking about.
- Create a Crypto Investment Plan – See Section #2.

SECTION #2: How to Create a Crypto Investment Plan

The very best way to avoid emotional extremes is to create an investment plan. No matter what the market is doing or what the headlines are saying an investment plan is the roadmap you'll follow in any type of market.

An investment plan can be as simple or as complex as you want to make it. However, getting started, the simpler the better. So, let's take a look at what a simple investment plan needs to consist of to help you get started.

An investment plan will provide you with an outline of the following:

- What is your investment criteria?
- What is the Asset allocation of your portfolio?
- Why you are investing?

Again, the key to successful crypto investing is to have a plan. Setting the right goals is vital to investing success. If you don't have a plan, how will you know if you're successful or not?

Prior to getting involved with cryptocurrency and blockchain technology in 2013, I spent 15 years as a registered investment advisor, series 7 stockbroker and mutual fund wholesaler. I had a number of clients that were millionaires and several multi-millionaires. I helped to construct investment strategies and portfolio allocation for individuals, families, business owners and professional athletes.

I also helped clients create investment portfolios for retirement planning, multi-generational investing and for current income. No matter how much money an individual had to investment I always started within the context of a personal investment strategy and risk tolerance.

Similarly, it's crucial that crypto investors have an understanding of the nature of overall risk in their portfolios and its implication on their ability to meet their investment goals.

Basically, investors only invest for two reasons. These reasons are for wealth accumulation and wealth distribution. These are two completely different approaches. In crypto investing, the goal is always toward wealth accumulation.

However, as the crypto market continues to grow, some innovative development teams are now offering the ability for specific coins to out pay dividends. To learn more about creating an income orientated component for your crypto portfolio, check out the resource section at the end of this book.

When building a crypto portfolio, risk is defined as the volatility in your portfolio. Volatility doesn't translate into loss but it only increases or reduces your ability for wealth accumulation.

The only time a crypto investor would lose money is when they sold out of their position below the value of their initial investment into the position. For many in the crypto world, losses are caused by making rash decisions to sell during extreme moments of volatility.

Investing is more about mental discipline than it is about selecting the next hot crypto. There will always be price movement, but as a crypto trader, the best way to increase your probability of success when opening a position, holding a position or closing a position is to follow your investment plan.

Creating a Crypto Investment Plan

Let's turn our attention to learning how to create a crypto investment strategy. A crypto investment strategy consists of four components:

- Risk Tolerance
- Wealth Accumulation Goals
- Performance Expectations
- Taxes

When I work with my crypto coaching clients, assessing risk tolerance is one of the most important component of creating an investment strategy. It is as much an art as a science.

Use the list of questions below to help you determine your individual risk tolerance:

Defining Your Risk Tolerance

What is Your Current Age? _____

What is your time horizon? (When do you expect to withdraw cash from your portfolio?) _____

What is the source of money to fund your crypto portfolio?

- Earned money from your daily income – This source of money tends to be a more conservative allocation.
- Windfall money – This source of money tends to be a more aggressive allocation.

Do I feel comfortable with 10% - 30%+ daily fluctuations?   Y or N

How would I feel if I woke up tomorrow and the value of portfolio was down 25%?

- Very stressed
- Somewhat stressed
- Not stressed
- Would feel very low stress and would consider investing more

When it comes to my experience in investing in crypto, I would describe myself as...

- Very inexperienced
- Somewhat inexperienced
- Somewhat experienced
- Experienced
- Very Experienced

During active market declines, I would sell my cryptos and reallocate my portfolio to a fiat (cash) position.

- Strongly agree
- Disagree
- Somewhat agree
- Agree
- Strongly agree

Now that you have completed your questionnaire take time to review your responses. Your answers will help to give you a better understanding of your individual risk tolerance.

Wealth Accumulation Goals

Wealth accumulation goals are attached to the "why" you are investing into crypto in the first place.

Why you are investing into crypto is a question only you can answer. This section of your Investment Plan focuses on the "why" and not on the "how".

The *why* you are investing is more important than the *how* you are investing. The *why* will give you the motivation to learn about the cryptocurrency realm before you invest one dollar. It will keep you up at night, in a good way, learning and reading about cryptocurrencies, Bitcoin and the blockchain. The *why* is the motivation to get up early to take this course and stay up late to restudy this course so you make sure you learn everything in it.

Use the questionnaire below to help you define why you are using cryptocurrencies as an investment. What is your end goal?

Wealth Accumulation Goals Questionnaire:

I am investing into crypto because:

- I want to quit my job in _____ months?
- I want to:
    - Buy a new house
    - Renovate my house
    - Buy a new car
    - Take a dream vacation
    - Support my parents/kids
    - Support my favorite charity
    - Pay for college
    - Obtain a comfortable lifestyle
    - Insert additional choices on the next several lines:
    - _____
    - _____
    - _____
    - _____
    - _____

Does Your Current Lifestyle Support Your Crypto Goals?

Just because you invest into cryptocurrency it doesn't mean you'll get rich. Is it possible Yes, but everyone has a different definition of rich. For some people, $10,000 in a crypto portfolio is rich, while others want nothing less than $100,000. You need to define from where you are starting and set realistic goals based upon the opportunities the market presents.

Your current lifestyle will have a substantial impact on how you trade your crypto portfolio. For example, if you work in an office where your boss doesn't allow employees to visit personal sites during the day, you can't keep a constant eye on the market. You can't take advantage current opportunities. Keeping this is mind, adjust your trading capability to your lifestyle.

Let me explain, if part of your wealth accumulation strategy is to day-trade, but your current work environment doesn't allow you access to your crypto account during work hours. This means you may be setting yourself up for increased levels of emotional stress. Your current lifestyle is in conflict with your ability to day-trade. Experiencing this situation, it may cause you rush trades and make irrational decisions since you only have limited time to keep a constant eye on your account.

Or, if you are in a personal relationship and your other half doesn't support you in your trading crypto. This situation too, may lead to increased stress levels.

When trading, be realistic with your expectations and your goals.

Performance Expectations

To be realistic, the real dollar returns available in crypto are astonishing. Coins can go up 100%+ with hours and the same coins can fall back almost 100% in a very short time, too.

Can you earn 100% within a week? Yes! Could it happen to your portfolio? Yes! However, don't build your expectations around the 100% return goal. Build your portfolio expectations for your individual investment time horizon and your current lifestyle. Focus on making small but consist gains.

Crypto investors who chase prices usually find themselves buying at the top. They end up buying high and selling low. If that happens often, you won't have much of a portfolio to work with in a very short time.

Paying Taxes

The purpose of this section is not to offer tax advice. It is only to remind you to consult with a tax professional regarding any tax liabilities in relation to your crypto trading.

What is your Investment Criteria?

The first set of decisions you need to make before you begin to trade is what are the types of cryptos you will be trading. In other words, what is your investment criteria?

This is the mandate you will stick with when selecting cryptos to trade. Regarding each crypto you are considering, use the list below to begin creating your personal investment criteria:

- What is the market capitalization?
- Does the cryptocurrency have whitepaper?
- Does the cryptocurrency have a roadmap?
- When was the coin created?
- How skilled is the development team?
- Does the development communicate regularly with the community?
- Is the website professionally designed?
- What is the social media presence? – Facebook, YouTube, Reddit, Telegram, etc.
- Does the coin solve a real-world problem?
- What strategic partnerships have been achieved?
- What exchanges can the coin/token be purchased on?

Make the decision to only invest into coins AFTER you have completely answered all of the questions above.

For example, you may decide to only consider investing into coins/tokens ranked in the top 50 market capitalization as defined by CoinMarketCap.com.

In addition, you may decide that development team communication is vital to you. Thus, you will only consider coins/tokens in which the development team communicates with the community at least every two weeks.

The development team can use Facebook, Twitter, Telegram, forums, etc. It doesn't matter how they keep the community updated, but how often they communicate. A well-engaged development team is a strong indicator of future success.

Creating your investment criteria does take time, but the effort is worth the return.

How to Create the Best Portfolio Allocation for You:

The first step in creating a portfolio allocation is to follow the ***Crypto Investment Pyramid***. It offers diversification by using a 3-tiered approach to investing.

The philosophy of a 3-tiered crypto strategy is simple. This strategy emphasizes diversification, flexibility, capital appreciation and is able to accommodate your risk tolerance. Below are the three tiers of crypto investing pyramid:

Tier 1: Blue Chip Cryptos:
BTC (Bitcoin), LTC (LiteCoin), XMR (Monero), ETH (Ethereum), DSH (Dash), etc. These are coins in the top 20 positions of market capitalization, solve a need in the marketplace and have a long track record of success. (50 – 60% allocation)

Tier 2: Penny Cryptos:
ADA (Cardano), BAT (Basic Attention Token), XLM (Stellar), etc. Lower priced coins with good technology, good management teams and solve a need in the marketplace. (20 – 30% allocation)

Tier 3: ICO Initial Coin Offerings:
An ICO is similar to an IPO (Initial Public Offering). This is how development teams raise money from investors before a coin is available to the general public. These are the highest risk since you are investing your money into an unproven coin, an unproven management team and unproven technology. (5 – 10% allocation)

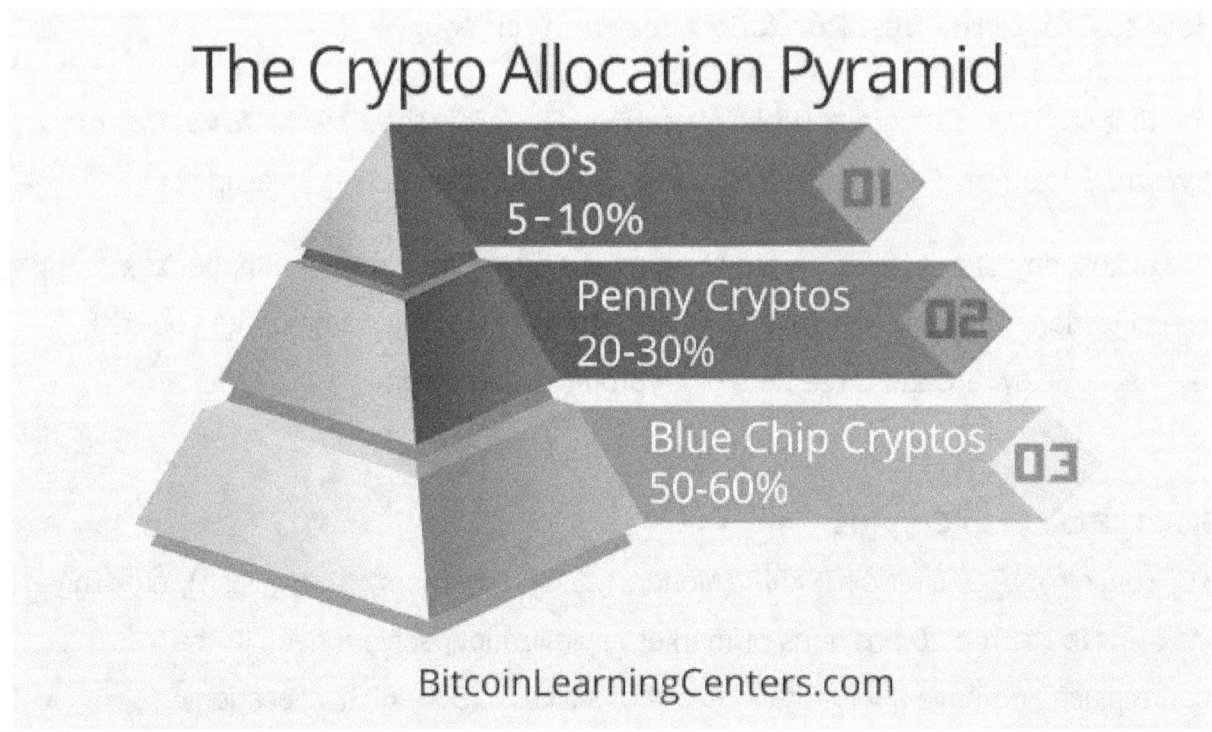

Now that you have completed your Crypto Investment Strategy, in the next section you'll learn to have the right mindset to make consistent returns on your portfolio.

Key Takeaways:

- Consider your current lifestyle when determining how much time you can realistically spend trading your crypto investments.
- Keep your performance expectations realistic.
- Your investment criteria will help you to make decisions on what type of cryptos to invest in.
- Different capitalization cryptos help to diversify your portfolio.

Suggested Actions:

- Set aside time to create a comprehensive investment plan

SECTION #3: How to Trade Without Emotion and Make Consistent Returns

Unchecked emotions can cause crypto traders to throw aside the concept of risk or trade in very large positions. Thus, offering the potential for very large losses.

Emotional trading is rooted deeply in the emotions of fear and greed.

One of the common threads I see with my crypto coaching students is many traders tend to trade in large volumes. Upon further examination, the reason for taking a large position can be linked to the fear of missing out of a huge potential price spike.

When I first consult with my new students, one of the first questions I ask is:

"On average, how much of your total capital do you commit to a single trade?" The answer I hear most of the time is between 50% to 100%. In the crypto market or in any market, going a 100% in a single position is a huge mistake.

Also, having 50% of your portfolio in a single position is a huge mistake. 25% is a huge mistake for one trade. Remember, to be successful you need to be consistent on the percentage of return and not as much as the dollar amount of a trade.

Again, it is the percentage of return of you make on each trade, not the dollar amount, that makes you a successful trader.

If you are a beginner and are not sure what to do, please follow this very simple rule which will save you in the long run:

MAKE YOUR TRADES SMALL

I am talking stupid small. Make your positions so small that you won't notice much of a dollar gain when you reach a profit. At this point, you may be asking yourself, "why have a trading strategy if you're not making a lot of money? If it is not fun, why trade?"

For example, if you have $10,000 in your trading account, you should only have 5% - 10% in any single coin.

Small trades will help you to be more objective when exiting a trade as well as staying in a trade longer. Being object allows you to focus on the reason to exit the trade when the market supports the right reason and time to exit.

In addition, having a smaller position allows you to focus on the current momentum and trend in the market allowing you to stay in the trade longer. You won't be focusing on the dollar amount, but the reasons for staying in the trade.

Treat trading like a business not a game. A lot of people approach crypto trading like a day at the casino. If that is your approach to crypto trading, let me ask you a question: Who usually wins at the casino? Is it the player or the casino? You already know the answer to that question.

Also, when you're trading small, you will only profit small. However, when you have a losing trade, you will only lose small. Doing this, you'll learn to trade without emotion. In addition, without emotions involved, you will be able to analyze your trades, be able to set your entry and exit points, make logical moves and follow your investment plan and achieve your investment goals.

Then, simply repeat this small trade approach 100x or 1000X. Remember your goals is to be a long-term, consistent crypto trader. Have patience and following your plan and you'll have a great chance of success.

If You Can Make Money in Small Amounts, Then Why Are Many Traders Impatient?

Believe me, I get it. Crypto offers an opportunity to make a lot of money in a very short amount of time. Taking this into consideration, here are the more popular reasons why so many traders are impatient:

- They dream of massive gains that can be achieved in a short amount of time. So many traders are in a hurry to make money.
- They have lost money in the crypto market and are trying hard to get back to breakeven point with their initial investment.
- Trying to reach a specific financial goal (buying a new car, paying off debt or paying rent).
- They think crypto is the ticket to become a millionaire in a very short amount of time.
- They read how others are making massive amounts of money and feel they are missing out. However, the majority of traders lose money consistently. Unfortunately, once you start losing money in trading, as all traders do, the pressure to make the money back, causes many to have no patience and they start making rushed and random trades. Thus, pushing them in the wrong direction.

In the long-term, making small, consistent profits will turn into large profits without the need to "play big" or "risk it all!"

The Worst Mistake Any Crypto Trader Can Make

The crypto market is one of the highest risk markets to participate in. You can make 6 highly profitable trades and the 7th one can literally ruin you. If your portfolio is made up of highly concentrated positions in only a few cryptos then your portfolio and your emotions can easily get crushed.

Let's turn attention back to the chart of Bitcoin from the beginning of November 2017 to April 2018. Bitcoin rose from about $6000 to nearly $20,000 and dropped back to $6,000. Just image if you started watching the market in December and decided to take a position in Bitcoin at the beginning of January at the price of $16,000. Within a very short time, the value of your portfolio tanked to about $6,000. It is a sad reality for many novice investors and those who rushed their trades.

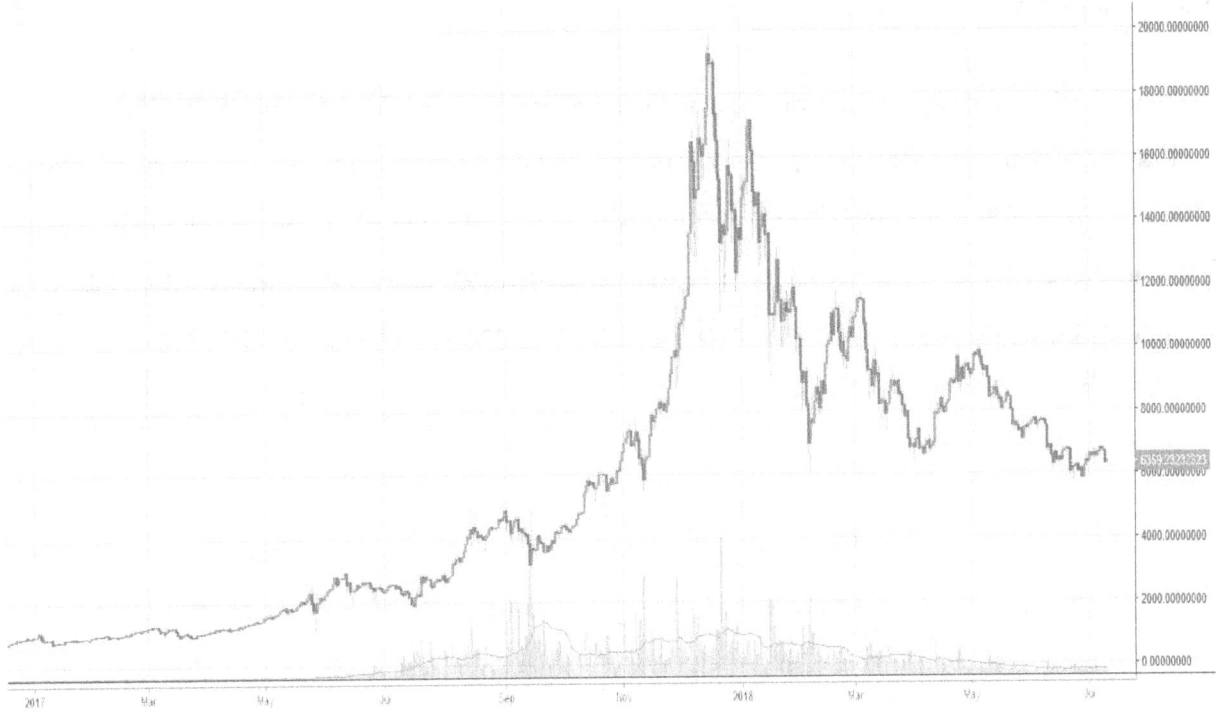

Market declines can lead to emotions that literally draw your life energy and can even negatively affect your physical and mental health. That is why managing your emotions is even more vital in most instances, than being the best technical trader in the universe.

Let me share a story about emotional trading with you from when I was an investment advisor during the late 1990's "dot com" boom and bust. I had a client that just received an inheritance from his parents. It was approximately $1,000,000 and he wanted to "play" the markets. After much discussion, I advised him to place take $50,000 from the inheritance and use it as "play money". Go buy a new car, do some remodeling to his house, take his wife and kids on a 5-star 14-day vacation. Basically, take a small percentage of the inheritance and do something with the money that you wouldn't normally do since it was an unrealized windfall to him.

With the remainder of the money, I would create a long-term, well-balanced portfolio to produce current income for his family and long-term, multi-generational wealth for his kids. At first, he agreed. However, after buying a new car, he called me and decided to follow a different strategy and invest the remainder into the market. At the time, the stock market was very hot.

Since he was reading articles on how others were making a lot of money trading options, he wanted most of his portfolio to be used to trade options. This would allow maximum leverage and maximum return. After several days of consulting with him and advising against this new strategy, I received a call and he told me he wouldn't be investing his inheritance with my guidance. He decided to open an account with another broker, he told me wanted to trade options and manage his own account without any guidance.

That was the last time I talked with this client. However, several years later, I was eating lunch at a local restaurant and his wife was also having lunch at the same restaurant. After talking with her, I found out my former client lost all of the inheritance while trading options. She told me soon after he lost the money in the market, he became depressed and angry. She ended up divorcing him and is now happily remarried with a new husband who also adopted her kids.

Having concentrated positions is like gambling, it is not trading. NEVER GO ALL IN!

How Much is Too Much?

In this section, I wanted to share with you what to do if you have made a mistake in your trading and now need to get back the investment you lost. The answer may surprise you.

The answer is not to begin trading in highly concentrated positions or trade more frequently. You don't want to keep doing the things that got you into the situation you now find yourself in. It is time to do something different. The answer to the question is:

- Don't chase the money you lost. The money is gone.
- Read, learn and regain your confidence in your trading strategies and learn new trading habits.

I know it is hard, but really try to think about *why* you lost the money. It wasn't the market that made you lose money; it was how you interacted with the market. Maybe you didn't fully understand the chart pattern you were reading. Maybe you made a decision to buy on a comment or tip you read in a forum or crypto chat room.

If your goal is to make that money back as fast as you can, you've already lost before you started. You're letting your emotions take over. Your goal should be to learn what made you lose money in the first place.

Take the time to reflect on why you placed the trade in the first place. Reflect back on the thought process you took prior to the trade. Take the time to restudy the charts and look at specific time on the chart you opened the position. Look for the following items when you review the price chart:

- Where prices hitting support or resistance levels?
- Did your market indicators give a buy or sell signal?
- Was the volume high or low?
- What was the overall trend in the market. Was the crypto market red hot or experiencing a bear market?

After taking the time to reflect upon your past trades, you'll start to see a pattern in your trading style. Once you have a better understanding of your past trades, you'll be able to make better trades going forward.

Think of the money lost as an experience. Something you paid dearly for and that will lead you to be a better crypto trader and investor. Here is how to get the most out of your past trading losses:

- Use it as a motivating force to get you to educate yourself to become a better chart reader
- Use it to help you better understand your emotions
- Use it as a catalyst to reexamine your investment plan

Finally, think about your financial goals and how living through both bull and bear crypto markets have provided you with a deep knowledge of trading. Make the decision to give it time, have patience, make small trades and sharpen your trading skills. Over time, you may find you'll be able to get back the money you lost. This will be something you will be very proud of.

Key Takeaways:

- Trading with high volume and concentrated positions will make you fear trading.
- When you are trading in concentrated positions and in high volume, small price movements will seem to be huge unrealized loss. You may be tempted to close them without following your predetermined trading strategy.
- Your emotions will add pressure to make more frequent trades in an attempt to get back what you lost. This could make you lose a lot of money very quickly.
- Remember, the market ALWAYS provides opportunities to make money. Why hurry?

Action Steps:

- Take time to review your last 10 trades and determine why you made the trade in the first place.
- Take time to improve your technical analysis capability. (Learn more about my technical analysis for crypto traders in the resource section)

10 Reasons Crypto Traders Make Money

When I first started in my investment career in 1994, only institutional investors and professional traders had access to fancy charting software and in-depth fundamental analysis that are commonplace in the crypto world today.

With all of the fancy charting, up-to-the-second price action and massive amounts of information, you would think the majority of crypto traders would be successful. The sad truth is many aren't. Many lose much of their initial capital within the first few months of trading, if not sooner.

In fact, most traders don't make any money. They simply provide liquidity for the few profitable traders. In fact, this isn't just for crypto trading, but all trading in general.

Unfortunately, many professional money managers who manage some of the largest mutual funds fail to beat the benchmark indexes they are paid to exceed for their clients.

In addition, many of the talking heads on Youtube have no professional training or financial background. In fact, I recently saw a YouTube crypto personality who produced over 50 crypto videos and over 25,000 followers state he has only been in crypto for the past 6 months. Seriously! Unfortunately, he has over 25,000 individuals following his "crypto advice".

Everyone is a genius in a bull market, but where are they during a bear market? It's during these times when their clients really need their guidance and experience. With my guidance you will have the knowledge to succeed through the various markets.

What makes a successful trader?

- It is IQ?
- Is it technical analysis or charting skills?
- Is it having the best trading software?

There are ten skills successful traders have that allow them to make money consistently.

Successful traders:

1. Have a trading plan. Their plan is well-defined. It has specific entries, exits, and position sizes before they make any trades. Unsuccessful traders don't have a plan. Without a plan, their results will be random and any profits made will be given back to the market.

2. Have an edge. Successful traders have knowledge. They do their homework about support and resistance levels. They watch and read the charts. They read the whitepapers of the coins they have an open position in.

3. Don't make highly concentrated trades. They don't place a trade that is too big for their portfolio. The reason they don't take big positions is because huge positions can cause emotions to infringe on reason and logic. Small price swings in large concentrated positions can lead to making irrational decisions.

4. Have the discipline to follow the plan they created.

5. Don't have to prove they are right, they want to make money. Unsuccessful traders won't admit when they made a wrong decision and sell at a loss. Unsuccessful traders illogically may let a small losing trade turn in to a big loss just to avoid admitting that they were wrong.

6. Let a small profit turn into a small lose because they know they are following their trading plan. Successful traders don't exit a trade until the trading goal is achieved or new information is introduced to the market that makes the

information used to make the trade outdated.

7. Use stop losses. Stop losses allow an exit point if the price action isn't what the trader thought it would be.

8. Constantly read about the positions they own. They listen to podcasts and interviews of the development team. They stay away from the chat rooms and troll boxes because many of the traders in crypto chat rooms and troll boxes are unsuccessful. Many are looking for tips on what to buy next. Successful traders stay away from the chat rooms and troll boxes without a reason.

9. Have a plan if they do participate in chat rooms and troll boxes. If a successful trader is spending time in a crypto chat room, they are there for a reason. Maybe it is to read the comments to see if they can find a hidden gem among the comments. I rarely spend time in the troll boxes, but on occasion I do quickly visit select telegram channels. When I am there, I quickly scan the comments for a crypto I may be unfamiliar with. For example, during a quick scan of comments in a troll box back in 2017 I read about PIVX. I wasn't familiar with this crypto before. After doing additional research I decided it met my investment criteria. Chat rooms and troll boxes can be valuable if you have a reason for participating in them.

10. Don't let their personal predictions or convictions rule them. While they may strongly believe in a specific crypto or the skills of the development team, it is the market that determines the future of any particular crypto, not the personal convictions of a single trader.

Key Takeaways:

- Create and follow your trading plan. Your plan should include the following:
    - Entry point
    - Exit point
    - Stop losses
- Don't try to guess on short-term price movement. Go with the market trend (sediment) and the overall flow of the market and price movement.
- If you're wrong, quickly admit it and cut your losses.
- Have an exit point in place during appreciating markets.
- Lock in profit with upwardly adjusting your stop losses.

Action Steps:

- Learn more about the following technical analysis including:
    - Relative Strength
    - On Balance Volume
    - Bollinger Bands
    - Moving Averages

Can You Predict the Future Price Movements in the Crypto market? The Answer will Surprise You!

In this section I will share with you how you can confidently predict support and resistance levels of many coins in the crypto market. I am referring to using technical analysis in the crypto market.

The big question I get from my coaching students is "Can technical analysis work in crypto?" From my 25 years of investment experience, any tool used for market analysis in the traditional market can be used in the crypto markets. The crypto market is not unique.

One of the greatest advantages to using technical analysis in the crypto market is everyone else is using it, too. The traders that are familiar with Fibonacci, Gann Fans, candle sticks, support and resistance and other main indicators are probably using them to chart their favorite cryptos. This means you can confidently predict price resistance and support for most cryptos. To learn more about technical analysis, check out the resource section in this course.

However, one thing to keep in mind in the current state of the crypto market is many coins that have low daily volume and can be manipulated. This happens in traditional markets too, especially in the penny stock market. However, technical analysis works best with the coins with consistently high daily volume, so stay away from low volume coins.

What is Technical Analysis?

Technical analysis is the methodology of forecasting future price movements through the study of past price movements, daily volume and past market data.

Technicians use many methods of attempting to predict current and future price movements using popular indicators, price chart patterns including support and resistance. These indicators help to assess if a crypto is trending and what is the probability of a specific crypto's ability to continue to trend in a specific direction.

Those who understand and use technical analysis in the crypto market have a huge advantage over those who are simply guessing or searching for tips from a crypto forum. Having even a basic understanding of technical analysis is vital to your success as a crypto trader. If you're looking to learn proven technical analysis strategies when trading crypto's, check out my Step-by-Step Guide to Crypto Trading Using Technical Analysis. You can learn more about my course in the Resource Section.

Key Takeaways:

- Understanding basic technical analysis can assist with long-term crypto trading.
- Technical analysis can assist with:
    - Helping you to select the best entry point
    - Helping you to select the best exit point
    - Showing if a crypto is trending

Action Steps:

- Learn about the leading technical indicators including:
    - Gann Fans
    - Fibonacci
    - Channels
    - On Balance Volume

The #1 Reason to Lose Money When Trading Cryptos

Too much activity or trading can ruin your trading capital fast. I see a lot of beginners being overactive. They are overtrading. I get a lot of messages asking "What do you think about XYZ coin. I think it is breaking out. Is now the best time to buy XYZ?" or "XYZ coin has dropped 15%, should I sell?" or "I just sold XYZ coin, when do you think I should buy again?"

Are You Overactive?

Overtrading leaves subtle clues. You simply need to look for these clues to see if you are overtrading your account. The reason behind overtrading your account can be traced back to a combination of trying to make fast money and the fear of missing out of an opportunity.

Check out these signs of possible overtrading in your account:

- Always watching the charts. You always have charts of your favorite crypto on your mobile phone or have several tabs on your browser open, all at the same time, so you don't miss out on a sudden price movement.
- You're in a rush to make money for an upcoming expense including paying rent, buying a new car or paying off debt.
- You're trying to recover money lost from previous trades.
- You're trying to catch a coin that is ready to spike and worried the price will spike without you.
- You're using technical indicators in your trading that you may not fully understand. Thus, you are placing trades with potentially faulty information.
- You read the forums and telegram groups looking for "hot tips" and then possibly act upon those tips to buy or sell.

- You're following the YouTube "Gurus" or other authors. Many of the YouTube personalities and crypto bloggers, etc., have little or no financial background and aren't actually making money in their portfolios.
- You are afraid to see red (unrealized losses) in your account. If you are following your predetermined trading strategy, you know price fluctuation is natural.
- Making trading decisions on videos from YouTube or information read in an article that is several days old.
- Making decisions to purchase based upon information from one trader's opinion and then reading comments or watching a video and taking the opposite action based upon another trader's option. Different traders have different strategies.
- Trading on multiple crypto exchanges while having multiple positions.

Why is it a bad idea to overtrade your account?

When you overtrade, you could be setting yourself up to make mistakes. The reason more frequent you trade, the higher the chances are you may set yourself up for a possible mistake. A mistake that could lose you a lot of money.

Key Takeaways:
- If you are overtrading your account, take a break and step away from trading for a few days.
- Stay away from day trading your portfolio and instead look for strong trends
- Make a plan and stick to it.
- Don't rush your trades.

Action Steps:
- Take time to create a solid trading strategy and follow it.
- Take time to improve your technical analysis skills.

Take the Money and Run....

The returns in the crypto market are astonishing. This is especially true to someone who has experience trading stocks on the NASDAQ or options. A 10% or 15% return in a year for a stock position is considered great. While options offer the opportunity to provide outstanding returns, it is nothing compared to returns in the crypto markets.

For example, check out the table below offering an overview of returns for stocks, options, forex and cryptocurrencies.

- **Stock Trading:** On average, smart day traders can expect 6% - 8% profit annually
- **Option Trading:** On average, smart option traders can expect 12% - 15% profit annually
- **Forex Trading:** On average, smart Forex traders can expect 16% - 20% profit annually
- **Crypto Trading:** On average, smart crypto traders can expect 100% - ? profit annually

That's right, 100% or more annually. The opportunity to earn 100% can achieved in a week, but it's not guaranteed. So right now, crypto is the place to be for anyone looking to take the risk to enjoy the reward. However, these amazing returns have a downside, too. Yes, you read that right. 100%+ returns have a downside, but only if you don't have a plan.

You see, many traders have made amazing unrealized profits over the past few years. However, that key word is "unrealized". Unfortunately, many didn't take the profits out and simply watched their gains dwindle.

For example, let's say your portfolio started at $10,000 and after a week of a hot crypto market, your portfolio is now worth $15,000. Inexperienced traders do one or all of three things:

1. They cash out the entire position and possibly lose out on additional upside the momentum in the market is offering.
2. They don't have a stop loss strategy in place to protect their unrealized gains. Thus, as the market declines their profit turns into a loss.
3. They didn't implement a Withdrawal Plan.

Let me explain...

How to Create a Crypto Withdrawal Plan

A withdrawal plan is consistently taking small gains from profitable trades. This means simply cashing out a percentage of your gains on a regular basis and transferring that money into your bank account. The market value of your portfolio will always increase and decrease. The question is, do you want to take those gains and deposit them into your bank account or do you want the market to take them from you?

I don't know about you, but I would rather have cash earned from crypto trading consistently deposited into my account, no matter how small, than have the market take them back.

Consider this example...

- Value of your portfolio on January 1st:
    - $10,000 (10,000 coins owned with each coin valued at $1.00)

- Value of your portfolio on January 15th:
    - $15,000 (10,000 coins owned with each coin valued at $1.50)

Crypto Withdrawal Plan:

Sell 10% of your unrealized gains: $5,000 x 10% = $500. Take this amount and deposit it into your bank account.

Here is the reality of this action:

- Number of coins owned on January 1st: 10,000
- Number of coins sold on January 15th: 334 (500 / 1.5 = 334 – rounded to whole number)
- Number of coins owned after the sale: 9,666 with a value of $14,499

After withdrawing $500 from your account, you still have a very sizeable position of 9,666 coins remaining. In addition, as you trade with the disciplined mindset strategies you learned in this course and by following the strategies in my technical analysis course, you could easily make up the coins you sold in very short order. Thus, taking your position back to the full 10,000 coins.

In addition, this approach also helps you to manage your capital gains exposure. For example, you sold the entire gain of $5,000 you would be liable for those taxes on the sale. By following this withdrawal method, not only are you managing your capital gains liability, but also letting much of your position remain intact for potential future growth!

Resource Section:

Bitcoin Learning Centers:

Complete step-by-step how to safely store Bitcoin and cryptocurrencies. In addition, you'll discover select the best crypto trading platform for you. Visit BitcoinLearningCenters.com.

Technical Analysis Strategies for Crypto Trading:

While visiting BitcoinLearningCenters.com make sure to check out the *Complete Crypto Technical Analysis Course*.

Crypto Trading Coaching Program:

If you're looking to learn market-tested crypto trading strategies, learn more at BitcoinLearningCenters.com